MW00826996

The Other Side of the Keyboard

Milton Jones

COLLEGE PRESS PUBLISHING COMPANY· JOPLIN, MISSOURI

Copyright © 2005
College Press Publishing Co.

Toll-free order line 800-289-3300
On the web at www.collegepress.com

Cover design by Mark A. Cole

Library of Congress Cataloging-in-Publication Data

Jones, Milton Lee.
   The other side of the keyboard : another look at instrumental
  music in the church / by Milton Jones.
      p. cm.
  ISBN 0-89900-918-2 (softback)
  1. Music in churches.   2. Churches of Christ—Doctrines.
  3. Christian Churches (Disciples of Christ)—Doctrines.   I. Title.
  BX7325.J66 2005
  264'.06602—dc22

                                           2004028820

Dedication

To my musical family who lives on both sides of the keyboard.

*Barbie, you sing like an angel. God only knows
the contribution that you have made in changing the way
so many of us worship and are drawn to the throne room of God.*

*Pat, you are a contagious lead worshiper. You are destined to be a
legend. I still can't believe how many instruments you can play.*

*Jeremy, you are truly one of a kind. You can play guitar
like Eric Clapton, you can scat sing like Louis Armstrong,
and soon you will be playing accordion like Weird Al.*

I'm sorry that I only play the banjo.

Acknowledgments

My thanks go out to the Northwest Church of Christ and the Shoreline Christian Church who exemplified the prayer of unity in John 17 and merged to be one. The selfless agendas of the leaders of these two churches are a model for reconciliation.

I am indebted to my friend and golfing partner, Rick Atchley, for the way you have inspired so many of us to put aside our differences to find our commonalities in Christ.

Shannon Kenee, you were a tremendous source of help and encouragement in the editing of this book.

Don DeWelt led the way for me. I am honored to be walking down a trail that he walked years before me.

My gratitude is also extended to Danny Corbitt, Tom Burgess, Victor Knowles, Scott Sager, and Dean Barham for their assistance in the development of this book.

Table of Contents

Introduction

*T*he Other Side of the Keyboard. What does that mean? The keyboard is the instrument that separates two distinct fellowships—the Churches of Christ and the Christian Churches. I've been on both sides of the keyboard and think that it is time for a family reunion.

There have been very few books written on the subject of instrumental music in worship. Most books take a negative approach to the use of instruments. Most of the people who are in favor of instruments simply haven't had the desire to write books on this subject. They think that it is not very important. This book is different because I have changed my beliefs. I had the conviction that instrumental music was wrong, and I no longer hold that opinion. As a result, there is a greater motivation for me to write since I have been passionate about both sides of the keyboard.

People who grew up in Churches of Christ tend to be "head" people. We must have an intellectual and rational justification for our practices. But something significant has happened recently among many people from my background. They no longer believe in their hearts that instrumental music is wrong. However, they have discovered that it is very difficult for us to change until we not only deal with our hearts but also with our heads. I hope this little book will give some justification for the heads of those who have already changed their hearts.

A recent publication examining this issue in the church described this change not as a trend but a tragedy. I don't think it is a tragedy. And whether any publication wants to admit it, it is a trend. Why does anyone want to know what I think about this subject? I'm not sure except that I get calls, letters, and e-mails daily wanting to know my opinion on the biblical approach to this issue. People whom I have not sought out keep asking for my help in understanding this issue. Certainly, some of my conversations have been negative. But most of the inquiries were from people who also wanted to change and honestly felt that what they had been taught was either wrong or incomplete.

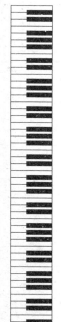

When I first addressed the subject of instrumental music in worship at my own congregation, I did not allow my talk to be taped. It wasn't recorded because I knew critics would want to tear my message apart. But this original message was for our particular congregation that was going through some unique changes. I wasn't trying to change the world or our brotherhood by that sermon. Now I have realized my naïveté in thinking that I could keep out of the limelight over this issue. Even on the night I spoke at our congregation, someone made a bootleg tape and a critic dishonestly put statements that I never said on the Internet. At least this book will actually be my words.

I'm not looking for any more debates. I'm not writing this book to argue with anyone. I've heard both sides of the arguments and studied them. I have simply changed. I believe that I'm biblical and am extremely happy with my position. I love the people who disagree with me. I totally

The Other Side of

understand what they believe and why they believe it. Even though everyone won't agree with me, I have found compelling reasons to change my stance on this issue. And I'm very convicted about my standpoint.

There are some churches and colleges who will think I have sold out. But I assure you that I didn't change my position by coercion. I simply believe that what I will present in this book is correct. For some reason I have been attacked by people not only locally but also from far away for the changes in my beliefs and practices. It is odd that people would attack me from far away when there are people in every city of other churches who use instruments. It reminds me of the situation in many Islamic countries. If you are already Christian, they will tolerate you. However, there is no toleration if you change from the Islamic faith to something else. That has been the case with this issue. It is very threatening to some in the Churches of Christ if someone in the Churches of Christ changes.

I also hope people in the Christian Church will learn something from this book. What I have learned from being able to hobnob on the other side of the keyboard is that people in the Churches of Christ are often called "stupid" because of their stance on instrumental music. That is not true, and it is not fair. There are some reasons for a belief in a cappella music. I don't expect people who read this book to leave their instruments and sing only a cappella music. But I would hope that you could at least understand that people in the Churches of Christ have rational reasons for their beliefs. Even if you believe that we have been misguided, I don't think it is fair or kind to conclude that we are ignorant.

When it comes to the style of this book, I decided not to take a scholastic approach. Instead I have tried to write it for the average person in the pew. I wanted to give a narrative approach of the progress of my thinking on this issue. It is my belief that a lot of people can identify with my journey. For a more detailed study of this issue, I recommend reading *Documents on Instrumental Music* by Tom Burgess and *Who Shackled Praise?* by Danny Corbitt. These books will be helpful if you need a study with more depth and documentation. I could have been more academic, but I felt as if I needed to write something short and simple for the people who are seeking some help aligning their heads with their hearts.

Chapter One
Experience

*T*wo worlds. One movement. Two fellowships. One body.

For the last two decades I've lived in two worlds. I have preached in a Church of Christ that sings a cappella. And I have taught in a college with the Christian Churches who worship with instrumental music. Both of these church groups have the same roots. They both are a part of a history called the Restoration Movement. But they split predominantly over the use of singing with instrumental music approximately a hundred years ago.

I grew up in a Church of Christ that didn't use instruments. My only church experience was in this environment. I was taught why we only worshiped a cappella, and I believed it. My conviction was not only that instrumental music was sinful but also that it was a matter of salvation. I know that sounds absurd to anyone who doesn't believe that way, but still it was the belief I inherited and adopted. My religious worldview was based upon being correct. If you were wrong on anything (at least a doctrine), you were in jeopardy of being lost. And our pivotal doctrine was instrumental music because it was a practice that gave my particular group a unique identity. No matter where you went, if you saw "Church of Christ" hanging over the door of the church building, you expected the music to be the same—a cappella. Without this unique belief, what distinction did we have?

Over the years, I mellowed on this issue (especially the part about it being a criterion of salvation), but I still thought instruments were wrong in worship settings. Although it was an issue that certainly wasn't central to the gospel, for some reason no other issue could cause more emotion. We couldn't go into any church that had musical instruments. If they had instruments, we would quickly get up and walk out in a fury. And we couldn't believe that others would so casually accept instruments, clearly disregarding biblical teaching (at least for us).

When I went to graduate school in Portales at Eastern New Mexico University, I discovered two buildings that were separated by a little walkway that was so small a person could just barely walk between the two buildings. One of the buildings was the Church of Christ Bible Chair. The other was the Christian Campus House. The Church of Christ Bible Chair was a place where members of the Churches of Christ taught college courses. The Christian Campus House was a place where members of the Christian Churches taught college courses. I had never heard of the Christian Churches before. They were from the same background as mine, the Restoration Movement. They believed nearly everything I believed, and yet it was as if they had not existed. At first, I thought they were the same as the Disciples of Christ but found out that they had divided from them decades ago. As a result, we either didn't know they were around or simply didn't talk about them. And here they were. Only a narrow passageway separated the two buildings of equal size. I took half of my classes in one building and the other half in the one on the other side. When I graduated with my Masters, professors from the Churches of Christ and the Christian

Churches had equally taught me. Remarkably, I never heard anything taught on either side of the passageway that was different. Yes, we believed the same thing. I was equally at home in either building. I'm not even sure if they disagreed on instrumental music; they only had a different practice.

Shortly after my graduate education, I moved to Seattle, Washington, to minister to college students at the University of Washington and at a Church of Christ. To my surprise, Dr. Glen Basey, the President of Puget Sound Christian College, asked me if I would also become a professor at his college. It was a Bible college to train students predominantly for ministry in the Christian Churches. I accepted. Again I found that I totally agreed with the faculty on nearly every issue. I found by being an insider that our two fellowships were nearly identical (in good ways and bad). Many of the faculty started attending the a cappella congregation where I was preaching. I also trained many preachers in the Christian Churches and began to speak at their congregations.

On one occasion, there was an attempt among churches in the Northwest to promote unity between the two groups. It was determined that the only way to bring us together was to have a debate and hammer out the divisive issue of instrumental music. Somehow I was selected to be the debater for the a cappella side. As a result, I decided to study the issue in the same manner that I had approached biblical issues in graduate school. I tried to lose my preconceived ideas and simply look at the Bible. Then I tried not only to read what Churches of Christ had to say but also what the Christian Churches and Disciples of Christ (the other part of our Restoration heritage) had written on this subject. When the debate occurred, I totally disappointed people from our side. Some said that I was more convincing for instrumental music than the guy from the Christian Church. But what I realized is that when I looked at this

the Keyboard

issue objectively, my previous arguments weren't really very convincing. I not only couldn't convince others, I couldn't convince myself.

This led me to see my movement as others saw us. For years, when people would visit our congregation, the first thing they tended to notice was that we didn't use instruments. So the first thing they would ask me was why we didn't use them. As a result, the first biblical discussion that I had with so many people was on the subject of instrumental music. Most of these people didn't hang around for other biblical discussions. Now I think I know why. Our arguments for not using instrumental music are not very convincing unless you already agree with that point of view or have decided that you already like our fellowship. If you don't already agree, they seem odd or as so many have told me— "stupid." And the real problem is that on most other biblical issues, I really have strong and persuasive arguments. But too many people never hear these discussions simply because the one that didn't make sense came first because it was so visible.

Gradually, through my experiences in graduate school and teaching as a professor, I learned what life was like "on the other side of the keyboard." And I liked it. They have always accepted me no matter whether I used instruments or not. Currently, I preach at a church that decided to actually live on both sides of the keyboard in one congregation. We have a cappella and instrumental services. Yet we are one church. We have shared leaders and ministries. But we worship in our assemblies in different ways. Recently, the Church of Christ and the Christian Church in our city decided to merge and become one. It seems to me that if we can do this in a congregational setting, we should be able to do it as a movement. We give each other the freedom to worship with or without instruments in our congregation with-

The Other Side of

out judging each other. We do it noncompetitively and accept each other.

Our congregation is listed in the directory of Churches of Christ in the Northwest. It is over a hundred years old. But when you see the list of Christian Churches in the Northwest, you can also find our name appearing there representing a congregation that is over 50 years old. I'm glad to be listed on both sides of the keyboard. We try to participate in activities, meetings, colleges, and mission efforts among both groups.

I now live on both sides of the keyboard. I love to worship either way. I equally consider myself a part of the Christian Church and the Churches of Christ. And I equally love each group. I truly think there can be unity between the two groups because I have experienced it. Our division is nearly a hundred years old. Isn't it time to get back together? Our movement was born out of a desire for unity and has divided over and over again. I would love to see, in my lifetime, churches uniting as they did in the infancy of our movement.

the Keyboard

Chapter 2
Interpretation

I like to take my Bible straight. That's certainly the way I've always prided myself. I follow the Bible and nothing but the Bible.

One day a church leader told me that every church must have either a creed or a hermeneutic. What does that mean? A creed is a document that a church council, denomination, or group writes to express their particular brand of beliefs. It is the doctrinal stance of their unique fellowship. It is not a statement to be contrary to the Bible, but it is a document to describe how they will practice certain biblical elements and what one must accept in order to be a part of their group.

A hermeneutic is a principle of interpretation. It is a big word that goes back to the Greek god, Hermes, who was the interpreter to the other gods. Even if you don't have a creed written down, you still have to interpret Scriptures. In the past I believed that we didn't interpret the Bible, based on a belief that 1 Peter 1:20-21 prohibited interpretation.

> [20]Above all, you must understand that no prophecy of Scripture came about by the prophet's own interpretation. [21]For prophecy never had its origin in the will of man, but

men spoke from God as they were carried along by
the Holy Spirit (2 Peter 1:20-21).

However, this passage merely tells us that the Bible
itself didn't originate from an interpretation of a prophet.
On the contrary, it was God Himself who revealed the Word.
But one still must interpret the Divine Revelation. When we
interpret the Bible, I might be wrong and you might be right.
Or I might be right and you might be wrong. Or we could
both be wrong. But God's Word is still correct, and there
should be some approaches to interpretation out there that
lead us closer to the truth.

In my past I would say that I worship without instruments because I follow the Bible. The people who use instruments don't want to follow the Word (or so I said). However,
this is not true. Both groups genuinely want to follow the
Bible. They simply interpret some matters of the Bible differently.

Growing up in an a cappella background, I was never
taught that we had a hermeneutic or a principle of interpretation. We were simply taught the same way by everyone. We
considered our way of looking at the Bible as the only way to
do it. It was never questioned. Our interpretation was what we
believed the Bible said. If you didn't agree with our interpretation, we thought that you didn't believe the Bible. Our principles of interpretation were not written down. We were very
anticreedal. But our principles of interpretation were like an
oral creed. We knew it. We believed it. And we stuck to it.

All Churches of Christ may not have had exactly the
same arguments coming from identical principles of interpretation. But in my case, there were three overriding teachings. We were never taught their historical roots. They didn't
have names. But we believed them, taught them, and fought
for them as if they were the Bible itself.

The Other Side of

First of all, there was what some have called *pattern authority*. In this case, there was not a pattern for instrumental worship in the New Testament church. If ever documented, this interpretation was rooted back to the early days of the Restoration Movement. The belief was that to bind any biblical teaching, you needed "a command, example, or necessary inference." Historically, this is usually attributed to a similar teaching of the early Restoration Movement leader, Thomas Campbell, who was the father of the even more famous leader, Alexander Campbell. Others have tried to take its roots to John Locke, the philosopher of the Enlightenment, an 18th-century intellectual movement in Western Europe that emphasized reason and science in its study of human culture. But we didn't really care about its roots because it is how we truly saw the Bible. It was as if this interpretation itself was inspired.

When applying this interpretation to our problem, it all revolved around the word "example." We couldn't find a New Testament command. No one ever could give a good definition of "necessary inference," so the question was whether or not there was an example of instrumental music in the New Testament. We concluded that there was not.

Several questions arise to me now when looking back at this principle of interpretation. Did it actually come from the Bible? Or was it simply the one we always used based on our tradition? Obviously, it didn't come from the Bible. We could interpret from the Bible that this is our correct interpretation. But no matter how long we go around that circle, it was still an interpretation.

Here's another question—did this principle come from the time of the Bible or the early days of the Restoration Movement? More importantly, is it a timeless principle of interpretation used consistently over all ages and people groups? Whether or not it has been used again and again

over time is debatable, but certainly it was a popular way to interpret documents at the beginning of the Restoration Movement. During these formative days of our religious heritage, the Constitution was being written in our country and interpreted according to comparable principles. As a result, it is only natural that the popular methods of interpretation of the times would be used in other venues. So a hermeneutic similar to the one being applied to the laws of our land was also used for the Bible. But the problem is that the Bible is not a constitution. In fact, it contains multiple genres of literature. And all kinds of difficulties start emerging when you use a constitutional interpretational method on a different style of literature like the Gospel of Matthew, much less the book of Revelation.

The pattern principle is further confused by its practice. Even if we buy into this interpretation, we still don't consistently apply it. Do we really follow all the examples of the New Testament? Think about head coverings for women, speaking in tongues, the holy kiss, and raising hands in prayer. All of these are examples, and most of us don't practice them. Other times we have practices where there is no example. We don't have examples for the kinds of church buildings most of us have, the songbooks we use, or the special church programs we offer in many of our congregations.

No, we tend to be inconsistent in how this principle is applied. It would be held up to rigid scrutiny if one proposed the addition of an instrument in a church assembly. But no argument would be thought necessary for most of the other items in our church buildings during assemblies.

Possibly a better way to deal with biblical examples would be to see them as a way you can do something. If the Bible gives a pattern, you now know a certain way you can practice a teaching. But to say that the example absolutely restricts you from practicing it any other way would be going

The Other Side of

too far. No one in any church consistently practices this prohibitive type of interpretation. They only put teeth into it on their pet peeve issues. In other words, if you cross the line on my big issue, I call out the violation of the pattern, but if it is not a big deal to me, I will cut you some slack.

The second principle of interpretation I was taught has often been called the *Law of Silence*. This principle means that if the Bible is silent about something, it is prohibited. As a result, the New Testament doesn't specifically prescribe the use of instruments. Therefore, since it is silent, musical instruments can't be used. It is a pretty simple argument. But again, does the Bible itself prescribe this interpretation?

Probably a better question is how do you interpret the Law of Silence? This has been the difficulty. I have seen both groups on both sides of the keyboard hold to this principle and arrive at totally different positions. In the Churches of Christ, we interpret the silence to be prohibition. If the Bible is silent, you are prohibited from doing anything else. However in the Christian Churches we have interpreted the silence to be freedom. In other words, if the Bible doesn't specifically tell you how to apply a teaching, you have the freedom to practice it in various ways. But in reality, neither group practices their view with complete consistency. Churches of Christ have always done things in other areas where the Bible is silent. And Christian Churches have not allowed total freedom to the point where anything goes when the Bible is silent.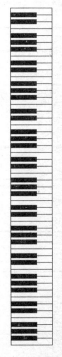

It is evident that this particular method of interpretation doesn't settle the matter even if we all agreed to it. For Churches of Christ, silence means you are prohibited from using instruments. For Christian Churches, silence means you are free to use them.

Another interpretation that I inherited was the *Law of Exclusion*. This simply meant that if a matter wasn't mentioned in the New Testament, it was excluded. Since singing was mentioned but playing an instrument was not, instrumental music is excluded.

J. W. McGarvey explained: "The instrument was used in the Old Testament worship but was never carried over by the apostles into the New Testament church and by the silence of the New Testament should be excluded in the same way burning incense and putting preachers in robes ought to be avoided because they were never included in the New Testament church which the disciples were seeking to restore. To introduce any item which was not introduced by God would be to set our own will to worship."[1]

This really sounds good, but it isn't the way we interpret things in our real world. As an example, if I were to say that I'm going to hear Willie Nelson sing tonight, does that mean he is not going to play his guitar? Of course not. In our everyday usage of language, to mention the word "sing" would not mean the exclusion of playing an instrument.

So what is our hermeneutic? Do we have one? We have certainly used one in my background. But we have never voted on an official one nor will we.

Other interpretations have been created in recent years called "new hermeneutics." Some say that there is a new hermeneutic in Churches of Christ today that has been adopted by some and divided over by others. But if there is a definitive new hermeneutic, I have never seen it.

At one of the unity forum meetings in the Restoration Movement, a different hermeneutic was presented that I liked better. Instead of "command, example, and necessary inference"—it was "command, principle and Divine indifference." Applying this method of interpretation would mean that we obey all commands, follow all of the eternal principles, and believe that some things don't matter one way or the other to God. This type of hermeneutic would be more

The Other Side of

conducive to a fellowship where instruments can be used either way in worship assemblies.

In a postmodern world that is less concerned with deductive reasoning, the most important element of this principle is the latter part—Divine indifference. The majority of people not rooted in this type of interpretation simply conclude that it doesn't matter to God if we use instruments or not as long as we worship Him from our hearts. As a result, the only question needing to be asked for most postmodern Christians is, "Does the music lead me to the one true God?" If the answer is yes, then that would be all that needs to be answered.

The fact of the matter is that we are never going to have an agreed-upon hermeneutic, much less a creed. Most Christians do agree on some basic hermeneutical principles, but do we really want a single authoritative method of interpretation? A lack of definitive rules of interpretation may seem scary, but in reality, it is good.

Rick Joyner explains:

> There is a God ordained ambiguity preventing the establishment of an absolute law or method of Biblical interpretation. This ambiguity is designed to keep us dependent on the Holy Spirit to lead us to truth. That men would presume that they could develop a system, or principles, by which they can interpret the Scriptures, is in itself an act of profound human arrogance. Such principles try to lay the burden of interpretation on a science in place of the Holy Spirit, which is itself a departure from the nature of true Christianity—a relationship with God. If such a thing were possible, why are they not clearly laid out in the Scriptures, and why do the writers of Scripture themselves so often depart from these principles? As stated, there are some principles that can help us in

our quest for Biblical truth; but there are no absolute laws or methods of Biblical interpretation. When we presume to substitute our own science for the Holy Spirit, we have by that fallen into serious error.

The Scriptures contain many paradoxes because the truth is found in the tension between the extremes. Only the Holy Spirit can enable us to discern such truth and keep us in the proper balance between the extremes that will cause us to depart from the course. Does this not open the doors for a great deal of subjectivity in interpreting the Scriptures? Yes! And that is the point. True Christianity promotes an extraordinary liberty for the personal quest of God's truth, a liberty that is required if we are going to believe from our hearts and not just our minds.[2]

There's a difference of interpretation on the other side of the keyboard. But is the distance between us bigger than God? And have the principles that have divided us truly come from God? When it is clear that Jesus calls us to unity and that our methods of interpretation have consistently produced disharmony, isn't it time for a reexamination?

Chapter 3

The Bible

My favorite "Peanuts" cartoon of all time has Charlie Brown talking to Snoopy who is seated on his doghouse pecking away at his typewriter, composing a new book. Charlie says, "I hear you're writing a book on theology." Then he adds, "I hope you have a good title."

Snoopy replies, "I have the perfect title."

Then Snoopy types out his title—"Has It Ever Occurred to You That You Might Be Wrong?"

It certainly never occurred to me that I might be wrong on the subject of instrumental music. For decades, I never questioned the belief or entertained any inkling of doubt about my position. My position was the biblical one. To me everyone else didn't really care much about the Bible. I honestly believed that if they would only believe the Bible more, they would agree with me.

But now it has occurred to me that I might have been wrong. In fact, I am convinced that I was mistaken.

Probably nothing in my past came across more insensitively as when I told someone who used instruments that they weren't biblical. It was the ultimate closer: "You just don't care about the Bible," or "You simply don't want to be biblical." In reality, I have never known or heard of a person who decided to use instruments because they don't want to follow the Bible. Every person I know from any church background who uses instruments does it because he not only thinks it is biblical but because he also wants to use all of his giftedness and creativity in worshiping God. It is not a question of whether one wants to be biblical; it's still a question of interpretation. Recently, a magazine said that I no longer followed the Bible because we have instruments at our congregation. I can't think of anything more incorrect. I am totally trying to follow the Bible and have never been more concerned about what the Bible says. In fact, I think my new viewpoint is more biblical, not less. But since the issue is called "Bible," we have to examine this.

What about the Old Testament? Musical instruments were used in Israel's worship throughout their history. They are mentioned numerous times. I can't think of a better example than Psalm 150.

> Praise the LORD.
> Praise God in his sanctuary;
> praise him in his mighty heavens.
> Praise him for his acts of power;
> praise him for his surpassing greatness.
> Praise him with the sounding of the trumpet,
> praise him with the harp and lyre,
> praise him with tambourine and dancing,
> praise him with the strings and flute,
> praise him with the clash of cymbals,
> praise him with resounding cymbals.
> Let everything that has breath praise the LORD.
> Praise the LORD.

The Other Side of

This passage speaks of various kinds of instruments. And all of them are used to praise God. And they are used in the sanctuary. I've heard arguments that say that God was really against instruments even in the Old Testament, but that kind of interpretation stretches the text far beyond any reasonable interpretation. Even if someone argues for a cappella music in the church, it has always been beyond my comfort zone (even when I was against instruments) to say that instrumental music wasn't acceptable in the Old Testament.

What I have found interesting in my history with the Churches of Christ is that I have never heard Psalm 150 being read in a positive way. Never once do I recall it being read publicly. When I suggested its reading, I was always told that it would cause trouble and shouldn't be read publicly. So for all practical purposes, passages of Scripture that mentioned instrumental music have been eliminated from our Bibles by their nonusage.

Two other passages from Second Chronicles are noteworthy. When the ark is being brought to the Temple in the fifth chapter, notice what it says about voices and instruments. "The trumpeters and singers joined in unison, as with one voice, to give praise and thanks to the LORD. Accompanied by trumpets, cymbals and other instruments, they raised their voices in praise to the LORD and sang: 'He is good; his love endures for ever.' Then the temple of the LORD was filled with a cloud." (2 Chr 5:13). Did you see how it says that trumpeters and singers became one voice? I had always viewed instruments and singing as separate items, but in this passage they have become one sound, not two. And if there is any doubt about instruments being ordained of God, perhaps no passage makes it as clear as when Hezekiah is purifying the Temple and it is stated: "He stationed the Levites in the temple of the LORD with cymbals, harps and lyres in the way prescribed by David and Gad the king's seer

and Nathan the prophet; this was commanded by the Lord through his prophets" (2 Chr 29:25). Indeed, in the Old Testament, instruments were not only acceptable but also commanded by God.

Well, how about the New Testament? Instruments are pictured in heaven.

> I saw in heaven another great and marvelous sign: seven angels with the seven last plagues—last, because with them God's wrath is completed. And I saw what looked like a sea of glass mixed with fire and, standing beside the sea, those who had been victorious over the beast and his image and over the number of his name. They held harps given them by God and sang the song of Moses the servant of God and the song of the Lamb:

> "Great and marvelous are your deeds,
>   Lord God Almighty.
> Just and true are your ways,
>   King of the ages.
> Who will not fear you, O Lord,
>   and bring glory to your name?
> For you alone are holy.
> All nations will come
>   and worship before you,
> for your righteous acts have been revealed" (Rev 15:1-4).

Perhaps what is even more interesting in Revelation is that the condemned (represented by the City of Babylon) have instrumental music taken away from them, which symbolizes the loss of joy in eternal destruction:

> Then a mighty angel picked up a boulder the size of a large millstone and threw it into the sea, and said:

The Other Side of

"With such violence
 the great city of Babylon will be thrown down,
 never to be found again.
The music of harpists and musicians, flute players
 and trumpeters,
 will never be heard in you again.
No workman of any trade
 will ever be found in you again.
The sound of a millstone
 will never be heard in you again" (Rev 18:21,22).

But the passages in Revelation aren't talking about the church on earth. I would have always argued that heaven wasn't the church and couldn't be used to justify instruments in a congregational setting (even though it does seem strange that God would allow something in His heavenly home that He considers wrong in His earthly home). So can the church ever use instruments? There certainly seems to be a silence in the New Testament about instruments especially if you compare it to the Old Testament or pictures of heaven.

The two passages most looked at concerning singing in the New Testament are Ephesians 5:19 and Colossians 3:16.

"Speak to one another with psalms, hymns and spiritual songs. Sing and make music in your heart to the Lord" (Eph 5:19).

"Let the word of Christ dwell in you richly as you teach and admonish one another with all wisdom, and as you sing psalms, hymns and spiritual songs with gratitude in your hearts to God" (Col 3:16).

In my earlier viewpoint, I believed that these verses lent themselves to a cappella music because they didn't specifically command the use of instruments and the music is to take place in a person's heart rather than on an instrument.

Since the verses are silent on instrumental music, I concluded that it must be forbidden for New Testament worship.

However, as I progressed in my journey on this subject, I realized that there were other matters of silence that I practiced. In fact, I always insisted that there should be simultaneous congregational singing when, in fact, the passages in Ephesians and Colossians are not specifically talking about the whole congregation singing together at the same time. When I started thinking about it, there were no commands or examples of congregational singing of this type that I could find in the New Testament unless you counted Jesus singing with His disciples at the conclusion of the Passover meal. In 1 Corinthians 14:26 it is clear that singing was a person singing to others. In the passages in Ephesians and Colossians, Paul is not necessarily talking about singing to one another in a congregational setting. So what I discovered is that I had allowed myself freedom on congregational singing when it was not specified. But I had not given others or myself freedom on instrumental music simply because it was not specified. I had always used Alexander Campbell's comment about instrumental music being like a cowbell at a concert as justification for its omission. But I never let his aversion for using musical notation in hymnals stop me when it was not specified in the New Testament either.

But is instrumental music totally absent from the New Testament? In Acts 2 the early church was worshiping daily at the Temple where there were certainly instruments being played.

"Every day they continued to meet together in the temple courts. They broke bread in their homes and ate together with glad and sincere hearts, praising God and enjoying the favor of all the people. And the Lord added to their number daily those who were being saved" (Acts 2:46,47).

The Other Side of

But the most controversial argument on this issue has to do with how the Greek word *psallo* is defined. This word found in both Ephesians 5:19 and Colossians 3:16 is translated "psalms." When I went to my Greek lexicon and looked the word up, I was surprised to find that its first definition was "to sing (to the accompaniment of a harp)."[3] This was the same lexicon edited by Bauer (translated by Arndt and Gingrich) that I had used for all my other word studies in graduate school. How could I ignore the first definition? But then I remembered what I had been taught growing up. My Sunday school teacher and preacher had both emphasized that the meaning of this word had changed by New Testament times. They totally assured us that it no longer meant "pluck an instrument" when Paul used it. The example they used was how the word "lyric" now meant words to a song when initially it referred to something with a "lyre" which was a musical instrument.

My biggest problem with this reasoning is that I was being asked to do word studies on *psallo* differently from the way I did them on other words. When examining other words, I was told that the original meaning was critical for understanding a word's meaning. We fought hard to defend our point of view on baptism by insisting that the first meaning of the Greek word for baptism was "to dip or immerse." We had to admit that the meaning of the word evolved over time, but we argued that the mode of baptism should only be done according to the original meaning of the word. But when it came to *psallo*, we insisted that our practice could not be governed by the original meaning but only by the later one.

My difficulty with our reasoning greatly increased when I discovered that the word still was being used to mean instrumental music in AD 160 nearly a century after Paul had used the words in Ephesians and Colossians. In fact,

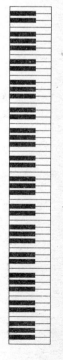

psallo was used in a writing that insisted that the word still meant musical instruments: Lucian writes, "for it is impossible to pipe without a pipe or to strum without a lyre or to ride without a horse."[4] The word used here for strum is *psallo*. From this text, it was held by this writer that it was not possible to *psallo* without an instrument in AD 160. It doesn't matter that this isn't a religious source. All that matters is that the word still meant musical instruments decades later. This is not what I had been taught. I admit that the word didn't exclusively have to be used for instrumental music. It had evolved to the point that it had multiple meanings, but it had not evolved to the point of excluding instrumental music.

Since Paul was not only a scholar but also inspired by the Holy Spirit, he knew the meaning of *psallo* could still be used for instrumental music. So why would he have used the word if his intention was to prohibit instrumental music? Paul would have known that Greek-speaking people would first think of instrumental music or at least know that it was a possibility by use of the word *psallo*. If using the word with a predominantly Jewish audience, he would have to know that they would probably first think of the Psalms which, as we have already noted, were songs used with instruments. If Paul had intended the prohibition of instruments, he would have never used a word that would have conjured up images of instruments with Jews and Gentiles. Or if he were going to use it and prohibit instruments, wouldn't he have qualified the word *psallo* with a prohibition to make it clear? Without a doubt you could argue that if he wanted instruments, Paul could have been clearer and mentioned instruments. But the other side of the argument is that if he wanted them prohibited wouldn't he have also been clearer? Weighing both sides of these arguments probably shows that Paul was not concerned with the very dispute we are discussing.

The Other Side of

Recently I was told that in a later edition of Bauer's Greek lexicon (edited by Gingrich and Danker), the first definition of *psallo* was changed to "sing, sing praise."[5] A cappella proponents loved this lexicon because it tended to lend more credence to their argument that the word didn't include instruments. This made me rethink the issue, but it still proposed a problem because this one lexicon didn't agree with many others that included instruments in the definition. (And isn't the reason that this particular lexicon was so heralded by my movement simply because it gave some authority to our own particular point of view?) And would God ultimately have us determine sin or wrong worship practices by which edition of Bauer's lexicon you purchased? Is God really that arbitrary? Do all the people before Danker changed the lexicon have faulty information for which God is going to hold them responsible?

Indeed, I think that Gingrich, the translator of the earlier edition of the Greek lexicon, made a profound comment when he was questioned on the meaning of *psallo* and the argument on whether instrumental music should be prohibited. He merely stated, "I must say that I regard the controversy over this matter as unimportant."[6] It is so obvious to any outsider that we have made more over this issue than is actually there.

And to prove the point further, Danker has once again revised his lexicon and stated that *psallo* meant, "to sing songs of praise, with or without instrumental accompaniment."[7] To make a case against instrumental music simply based on this word is again too arbitrary for my comfort.

Incidentally, those who wanted to hold to Danker's former translation that seemed to open the door for a case against the instrument never presented to me the reasoning for his change. He comments that there were two reasons: 1) the first-century Pharisees didn't like the instruments that

God had commanded of them, and 2) the early church didn't like the instruments used by certain idol-worshiping mystery cults.[8] Certainly these are reasons for not using instruments, but they are hardly biblical ones.

What does this entire chapter mean for us? I think those of us who have been on my side of the keyboard need to rethink the biblical position of instruments. Depending on how you define the word *psallo*, you not only could have an example of instrumental music in the New Testament, but in reality, also a command. But at least we have to admit that the silence is not as deafening as we have always presumed.

As a result, to say that one is not biblical simply because he believes instrumental music is acceptable in worship is not only unhelpful but also hurtful. And most of all, it is not remotely correct or honest with the plain biblical passages or the passages that are at least in question. To make acceptance of one another based on an issue as peripheral as instrumental music is regrettable. Certainly, some may argue that by writing this book I have made an issue out of something that is not actually central to what's important. That's probably a good point, and I apologize if the precise nature of this book draws people away from the true features of what should unite us in Christ. If someone says that the subject I have discussed is not important and is not at the core of Jesus' emphasis, I will understand that viewpoint. However, I have written this book to help the healing process, not simply to debate further what many, including myself, have come to believe is a marginal issue in Scripture.

Rick Atchley, when addressing the North American Christian Convention in 2003, prescribed the necessity of forgiveness to heal the wounds between the Churches of Christ and Christian Churches. He stated, "We are going to need to do some repenting and some forgiving. Now speaking from the a cappella side, it seems to me that we need to

The Other Side of

do most of the repenting and ask for most of the forgiving. But I'm sure some of you would say that from your side (Christian Churches) there have been some things said that would have grieved the heart of God too. . . . And I'm going to beg you—let's not let old wounds define who we are. Let's let the prayer of Jesus for one body define who we are."

I want to own up to his request, and I certainly hope that those to whom I've said hurtful and untrue words regarding their biblical convictions will forgive me of my unkind statements. And the beauty of it all is that I know these brothers and sisters have forgiven me. I also hope that if there are any who worship with instruments who have had a cavalier attitude or have written off a group of brothers and sisters simply because of a practice that seems odd to them will also repent and seek reconciliation. Is there someone on the other side of the keyboard you need to forgive? Is there somebody on the other side of the keyboard who needs to forgive you?

the Keyboard

Chapter 4

History

I've always thought the strongest argument for a cappella music in the church was historical. If you only use history, you could easily conclude that the early church did not use instruments when worshiping in the church. In fact, the meaning of the word a cappella is not, as most people think, "without instruments." In reality, it means "in the manner of the church" or "in chapel style." When people would hear music without instruments, they called it a cappella simply because it resembled the music you would hear in the church.

When did instruments start being used in church history? I'm not really sure. Growing up in the Churches of Christ, I was taught initially that it wasn't used until AD 1250. Later I learned from others in our movement that instruments were added in AD 776. In other histories of the church outside of my background, I heard of musical instruments being used as early as AD 324. When the Great Schism occurred in the eleventh century, there was a huge division in Christendom that resulted in the separation of the Orthodox Church from the Roman Catholic Church. Their histories did display a difference of opinion on the instrumental music issue. The Roman church used instruments in church assemblies, and the Orthodox Church continued in their understanding of the pattern of the early church and sang a cappella as they do to this day.

If only history is used to determine the practice of the church, a case can be made for a cappella music. But on the other hand, I was always taught to oppose arguments on other issues based primarily on historical precedents. The point of the Restoration Movement was to go back to the Scriptures rather than rely on what was done in church history. I was taught that the problem with the Roman Catholic Church was that they often based their beliefs on practices in church history rather than the Bible itself. Therefore I have always been hesitant to let the key factor for my beliefs be based on church history.

If those advocating a cappela worship are making church history the definitive argument for their practice, then they arguably have a stronger case. Admittedly, it seems that the early practice of the church was without instruments, even though it is still debatable as we saw in the last chapter with the examination of the church's meeting at the Temple and the meaning of the word *psallo*. But let's accept that the early church usually was found to be singing without instruments. If that is the case, then the big issue is, "Why?"

Some have suggested that the reason for the change is a theological one. In other words, some argue that there is a theological change taking place in the practice of believers from the Old Testament to the New Testament. As an example, the sacrifices that took place in the Old Testament are replaced by the one sacrifice of Christ in the New Testament. Obviously, there are some changes between the Old and New Testament. So was instrumental music one of them? It has been argued that the Old Testament focused on external

The Other Side of

practices where the New Testament centers on the heart. Certainly, there are some examples of this nature, but we have to be careful in this reasoning because it could lead to a viewpoint that God wasn't looking for a heartfelt faith but only a mechanical obedience in the Old Testament. There are too many passages in the Old Testament concerning the heart to go very far with that kind of thinking.

But to use this reasoning on New Testament passages means that if you sing with instruments, you aren't singing with your heart. If you don't worship with instruments, perhaps you could make that judgment. But anyone who has worshiped with instruments knows without a doubt that your heart is also involved in worship with instruments. I have worshiped deeply with my heart in a cappella singing. But I have to admit that my heart has been involved equally when I've worshiped with instruments.

The removal of worship with instruments in Christian times is also difficult to understand when it is obvious that it appears again in images of heaven. Instruments are used for praise in Old Testament times. They are included again in the picture of worship in heaven. So what is the reason for their removal for this brief age? Why were they not only acceptable but also commanded in the Old Testament, then prohibited for the church, and then pictured again for the eternally redeemed? There is no biblical or theological rationale to help us understand such reasoning.

Churches of Christ have always tried to make a strong distinction between Old and New Testament practice. However, one has to be honest that the circulation of the New Testament as a whole didn't happen in the first century, and the Old Testament was actually being used as Scripture for the church in the New Testament. If this was the case, the Psalms had to be used in the life of the New Testament church. If they were worshiping with the Psalms,

where would they have received teaching for the prohibition of instruments when the Scriptures they used actually encouraged it?

My current opinion on why the change occurred is because of the synagogue. People who attended an early synagogue service, according to my best examination, sang without instruments.[9] When we look in the book of Acts at the missionary strategy of Paul, it seems that he first went to synagogues and tried to bring Jesus into their practice. And it also appears that the early form of the church, as a result, was patterned after the synagogue. So why was the early church without instruments? Probably they simply kept the pattern that was their heritage. It's the same reason that I worshiped most of my life without instruments. It's the way I've always done it. Whether people feel comfortable singing with or without instruments is usually based more on how they grew up than whether it is right or wrong. Staying in your comfort zone is certainly a driving force for everyone's position regardless of which side of the keyboard you find yourself. Even as fighting has diminished on this issue and people are not wishing as much ill will towards the other side, many people still will like to do what they have always done.

I've heard it argued that we ought to sing without instruments because that is the way the synagogue did it. This reasoning simply doesn't work for me. The synagogue was never a prescribed biblical form. Certainly it was valuable, and God's people had the freedom to form synagogues for the continuation of the Jewish faith after the collapse of the Temple and the scattering of the Jews. But during most of the New Testament era, the Temple not only existed but also included the use of instruments. My point here is not that the Temple's form or style of worship ever became the pattern of the church, but it at least had biblically prescribed roots where the synagogue didn't. On the other hand, I don't

The Other Side of

think that it was wrong to adopt the form of the synagogue for worship assemblies. I only have a problem if someone tries to bind this form.

It wasn't until recently that I learned that the instrumental music controversy wasn't unique to the Restoration Movement. It was actually happening in the days of the early church. But it wasn't an issue of Christianity but of Judaism. The Pharisees were the leaders in the synagogues. Sadducees greatly influenced the events of the Temple. From the pages of the New Testament, we can learn that there were controversies and differences of belief between these two groups. One of their issues not talked about in the New Testament was instrumental music. In fact, some Pharisees wanted to eliminate instruments from the Temple because false mystery religions used them.[10] Another reason for the elimination of instruments was because of the rabbinical "fence" which prohibited the use of an instrument on the Sabbath because of the probability that it would require tuning or other preparation that would be interpreted as working on the Sabbath.[11] But it would be hard to side with the Pharisees in these arguments because they were arguing against the very practice that God had prescribed. It was God who set the pattern for Temple worship. I don't know how many sermons I have preached about where the Pharisees missed the heart of the matter. I don't think I want to go along with them here either. But we can see that the pattern of the church was similar to the pattern of the synagogue. The synagogue appears to be without instruments, and they did have reasons. It seems possible to me that the church either accepted the form of the synagogue or accepted their reasoning on this matter.

Another reason that the synagogue didn't have music I learned from one of my Jewish friends. He explained that instrumental music was eliminated from their worship after

the destruction of the Temple and the captivity of God's people. This is based upon the psalm that states, "By the rivers of Babylon we sat and wept when we remembered Zion. There on the poplars we hung our harps" (Ps 137:1,2). According to this view, instruments were signs of joy and were eliminated because of the destruction of Jerusalem. But he added that they were to be used again when the Messiah came. This gives another look at the reason for the omission of instruments in the synagogue. Their absence is not because instruments were believed to be wrong, but instead it was a type of fast until the Messiah came.[12]

My Jewish friend doesn't believe that the Messiah has come. I believe the Messiah is here. I want to celebrate in every way I can. I don't want to put restraints on my praise. I want to praise as they did in the days of Moses and as they will when they sing a new song of Moses and the Lamb. As a result, I'm willing to go to the other side of the keyboard.

Chapter 5
Entertainment

*T*hat's Entertainment!" is a good thing to say when evaluating an MGM musical, but in my heritage, not a worship assembly. It's another one of those closer statements. If it is entertainment, then it must not be worship and shouldn't be done. And over and over again, I've heard this description used to be a clincher for what's wrong with instrumental music—it's entertainment.

But before we slam the door on instrumental music, maybe we should decide if entertainment is wrong, if a cappella music could also be entertaining, and if the true nature of worship is music itself. The word "entertain" can be used in several ways. Certainly, it can be used in the sense of showing hospitality, as the Bible teaches us that we may be "entertaining angels unaware." But when it is used to mean, "the amusement or pleasure you receive from something or something performed for an audience," then that is where we begin to feel uneasy. Should something in a worship assembly give pleasure or amusement? In the past, I would say that it shouldn't. But on the other hand, I had no problem when the preacher was entertaining, keeping us amused (or even awake) by telling us humorous stories and making enthralling applications. In fact, I found myself complaining if he wasn't entertaining. It's not that I wanted to listen to him solely to be entertained, but I appreciated it when he brought liveliness to the message and kept truth from being seen as a boring proposition. I never left complaining that his sermon brought me some pleasure or amused me at times.

But on the other hand, there were times when I thought a preacher was calling attention to himself, perhaps for the needs of his own ego. Now that is a problem, but shouldn't it also be the issue with musical leaders? Isn't the critical issue the motives of the leaders and participants rather than the music itself? And couldn't a capella music be entertaining too? In one of the churches where I worshiped, they prohibited a lot of foot stomping, Southern gospel songs that featured bass leads and fast paces. Why? It was too entertaining, and we were singing those songs mainly because we liked the style and form rather than the message of the song. And it was true. The songs were entertaining. And it is equally true that any a cappella song leader can venture into the arena of entertainment by his behavior or call attention to himself with impure motives, just like an instrumental leader.

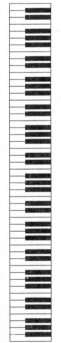

But whether it is a leader or anyone in an assembly, it is very difficult to judge another person's heart (only God can do this). And when we focus on trying to be the judges of other people's worship, there is probably something inadequate with our own hearts. There certainly needs to be a tolerance for worship on both sides of the keyboard if indeed it comes from the heart. And there needs to be an acceptance of each others' worship regardless of whether it is the style you prefer if it pleases God. To be real honest, it is just hard for me to believe that the heart of worship has anything to do with instruments or the lack of them. What's more, it is obvious that you can get your heart out of worship with or without

The Other Side of

instruments. You could be totally disengaged from the words coming out of your mouth with or without instruments. You could be totally concentrating on the notes of the music rather than the message with or without instruments.

In reality, entertainment in and of itself isn't wrong. And worship isn't something that only happens on a stage for an audience of people. Worship can happen any place where we give glory to God. Regardless of the kind of music, if God doesn't get the glory—worship doesn't happen. But any time God is glorified, whether on stage, in the closet, with or without instruments, in or out of a church building—worship occurs. And any time a leader is trying to call attention to himself rather than God, it's a problem. In a worship assembly God should be the audience, we should be the performers, and the leaders are merely prompters. Shifting attention to people rather than God is a problem, regardless of the form of music.

Matt Redman, one of today's most gifted and popular Christian musical artists, tells of his early days leading worship at his congregation in England. Their praise band became so popular that huge numbers of people started coming to worship with them. But the focus of the assembly started centering on the band too much. And as the band grew in popularity, they traveled more. As a result, people started inquiring about whether the band would be there that week before they attended. If a less popular band was playing, some people simply missed. In other words, some were coming just for the band, not for God.

As a result, the pastor of the church took some drastic action. He stopped the music. The band no longer played. They didn't do music anymore at church. When asked how long the music would be missing, the answer was, "indefinitely." By stripping all the externals away, the people started realizing what worship was truly about, and Matt

the Keyboard

Redman wrote a song in the "no music" period that has become a classic: "Heart of Worship."

> When the music fades,
> All is stripped away,
> And I simply come;
> Longing just to bring something that's of worth
> That will bless Your heart.
>
> I'll bring You more than a song,
> For a song in itself
> Is not what You have required.
> You search much deeper within
> Through the way things appear;
> You're looking into my heart.
>
> I'm coming back to the heart of worship,
> And it's all about You,
> All about You, Jesus.[13]

No matter whether you worship with or without instruments, the focus should be Jesus Himself. Certainly it is important to choose worship leaders based on their spirituality, not just their musical ability. Churches that are about to change from a cappella to instrumental music may too readily accept musicians because they are needed and not take the time to find leaders who bring people to the throne of God rather than to their own personal fan club. But even with all that said, a church shouldn't settle for boring or untalented musicians simply to avoid entertainment. The fact of the matter is that Jesus is not boring. Although He is holy, He is still very entertaining—and any music that will focus on Him long enough will at times be very entertaining.

Many people have equated worship with music or singing. In his best selling book, *The Purpose Driven Life*, Rick Warren states: "Worship is far more than music. For many

The Other Side of

people, worship is just a synonym for music. They say, 'At our church we have the worship first, and then the teaching.' This is a big misunderstanding. Every part of a church service is an act of worship: praying, Scripture reading, singing, confession, silence, being still, listening to a sermon, taking notes, giving an offering, baptism, communion, signing a commitment card, and even greeting other worshipers."[14]

A key problem is labeling music right or wrong depending on its style—because too often what is "right" is simply what we prefer. There are just as many worship wars among instrumental churches trying to decide what style of music to use as there are a cappella churches trying to decide if instruments are acceptable. And there are all kinds of worship wars in a cappella churches trying to decide between hymns, praise songs, and worship teams.

Again Rick Warren identifies the problem well:

> Even worse, "worship" is often misused to refer to a particular style of music: "First we sang a hymn, then a praise and worship song." Or, "I like the fast praise songs but enjoy the slow worship songs the most." In this usage, if a song is fast or loud or uses brass instruments, it's considered "praise." But if it is slow and quiet and intimate, maybe accompanied by guitar, that's worship. This is a common misuse of the term "worship."
>
> Worship has nothing to do with the style or volume or speed of a song. God loves all kinds of music because he invented it all—fast and slow, loud and soft, old and new. You probably don't like it all, but God does! If it is offered up to God in spirit and truth, it is an act of worship.
>
> Christians often disagree over the style of music used in worship, passionately defending their preferred style as the most biblical or God honoring. But

there is no biblical style! There are no musical notes in the Bible; we don't even have the instruments they used in Bible times.

Frankly, the music style you like best says more about you—your background and personality—than it does about God. One ethnic group's music can sound like noise to another. But God likes variety and enjoys it all.

There is no such thing as "Christian" music; there are only Christian lyrics. It is the words that make a song sacred, not the tune. There are no spiritual tunes. If I played a song for you without the words, you'd have no way of knowing if it were a "Christian" song.[15]

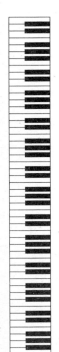

For many people from my background, a cappella music is our preference and love—and we simply don't want to lose it. The unique sound of a cappella music sung with four-part harmony in the Churches of Christ is not only our heritage, but it is also a thing of beauty. "With instruments we will lose four-part harmony," some have argued. But this fear has already been realized with the disappearance of hymnals and with computer screens projecting words without musical notation. Most young people have not only lost the attraction for four-part harmony, but also are not capable of it because of a lack of "passing the baton" from previous generations. We often forget that four-part harmony is only a recent innovation in the history of church music and certainly isn't the form of the early church.

My fear is that so many people in the Churches of Christ are hungry for a musical change that they will adopt instruments without thinking through the issue. If there is a change, it ought to be based on biblical teachings and belief. No matter how you land on the instrument issue, you should still be basing your beliefs on the Bible. Before our congre-

The Other Side of

gation changed its position, the leaders thoroughly studied the Bible and then I taught the congregation.

Some want instruments simply because they want instruments. That is really a selfish reason. A change should take place when there is the belief that it is biblical, that it is glorifying to God, and that it is a missional concern helping us connect the gospel with the outsider. It is imperative to quit making decisions in the church based on consumerism (what we would like or what they would like). However, it is important to make decisions based on mission (what will help people see Jesus and worship Him in our current world).

Instrumental music is not a quick fix for church problems. There will be some Churches of Christ who have not been growing that will think that all they have to do is add instruments and then they will reach people. That will not be the case. Randy Harris of Abilene Christian University said that those churches that think it is only about adding instruments will "die louder." Instruments or the lack of them is not the main concern of the church. Paul Colman, the Dove Award–winning Christian artist, led worship and then played a concert at the Northwest church. It was one of the greatest nights of worship I had ever experienced. I had goose bumps over and over again as I was simply moved closer to the presence of God. After the evening was over, Paul came up to me and said that he thought this was the best church he had ever seen. I expected him to tell me that we were so great at worshiping and singing since we had just finished our praise time. But instead he said that it was the best church he had ever seen because it supported more orphans than it had members. Paul had judged us by what was most important—not how emotional we were when we praised, but how loving we were when we served.

It is interesting to me how the Restoration Plea is not so unique anymore. You can find a church on nearly any corner that says it is trying to follow the Bible and seeking unity based upon the Word. Some of our distinctive pleas, like the Lord's Supper and baptism, are being restored in all kinds of different churches. But it is fascinating to me that none of these churches who are a part of a new movement of going back to the Bible have concluded that instruments are wrong. Could it be that the real reason for our use of a capella music has little to do with going back to the Bible?

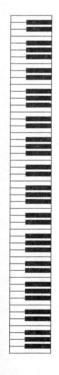

The Other Side of

Chapter 6
The Division

Any time there are broken relationships, there are stated reasons—and then there is the real reason. Finding out the real reason is often difficult to do, especially when it happened over a century ago. The division between the Churches of Christ and the Christian Church was recognized in the census of 1906. However, it had already occurred before that time. The census merely acknowledged what had already become a reality—the unity movement had divided.

Why did these two groups divide? Instrumental music, you could say. Without a doubt, that is true, but it is too easy of an answer. It certainly neglects other factors that helped create the controversy.

Culture was a huge factor leading to the division in our movement. It could be argued that we had a division based upon the differences in rural and city churches. The Churches of Christ were basically rural churches with rural worldviews. The Christian Churches were significant in the cities. This basically still holds true today. The largest church in the state where I minister is a Christian Church. In fact there are many large Christian Churches where I live. On the other hand, Churches of Christ have not had significant growth in large cities with the exception of a few cities in the South—especially in Texas and Tennessee.

As is nearly always the case, controversies among individuals are caused and driven by personalities. Over the years, individuals have arisen who focus on the issue and keep the controversy alive. It is still happening today. In the early years of division, there were preachers and editors who argued and debated over instrumental music and other controversies like the Missionary Society. Their opinions were heralded as central issues in our movement and put a wedge between the two groups. Benjamin Franklin and L.L. Pinkerton were two of the key Restoration preachers that argued and debated their positions on this issue. People tended to rally around one of the individuals. When issues get leaders, people always follow. There has never been a lack of people wanting to lead people away from the other group over this issue. As some of us are now moving toward unity and reconciliation, others will emerge to keep the arguments alive and people apart.

It could be argued that the Restoration Movement was looking for an issue to divide over. If it had not been instrumental music, it would have been something else. The driving vision of the Restoration Movement was twofold—going back to the Bible and unity. Is this possible, or do the themes lead in different directions? Richard Hughes states in his insightful look at our history, *Reviving the Ancient Faith*: "Instrumental music and missionary societies became divisive issues only after it became apparent that the Stone-Campbell movement had produced two irreconcilable traditions—one defined by ecumenical progressivism and the other by sectarian primitivism—and that the movement was in fact dividing along those lines. These two issues, therefore, functioned chiefly not as defining themes in their own right but rather as

The Other Side of

symbolic banners around which those who embraced these differing intellectual traditions might rally."[16] As David Edwin Harrell Jr. commented, if these people "had not disagreed over instrumental music and missionary societies, they would have divided over something else."[17] In other words the two distinctive themes of the Restoration Movement are hard to accomplish at the same time. When going back to the Bible is pursued, some may go farther than the intent of some passages. And if total agreement on every issue is demanded, a sectarian and legalistic system may develop that divides people every time there is a disagreement. This type of direction actually moves people away from the core ideal of unity. This has undoubtedly happened in the Restoration Movement as we have divided and splintered over so many peripheral issues. On the other hand, when unity is held as the paramount ideal, one may give up many long-held beliefs for the sake of unity. But this could move one away from the ideal of going back to the Bible. Toleration and acceptance become more important than mutual agreement on biblical doctrines. This was obviously seen in the history of the Restoration Movement in one of our other divisions where the Christian Church made a greater movement toward going back to the Bible and the Disciples of Christ championed a direction of unity and ecumenism.

Here's my opinion. I owe it to studying the issue with Dr. Harold Ford, who was one of the best church historians in the Christian Church and a former professor at Puget Sound Christian College. I think we had a significant division over the Civil War. You can't map it out perfectly, but if you try, you will find that the Northern or Midwest part of the Restoration Movement chose to be instrumental and the South was mainly a cappella. David Edwin Harrell concluded: "The most likely place to look for the sectional origins of

a church in the nineteenth century is in the wake of the bitter struggle centering around slavery and culminating in the Civil War."[18] Garrison and Degroot argue that there was no religious group with a greater per capita ownership of slaves than in our own movement.[19] How could this not be an issue? It is also interesting that there were differing viewpoints on the issue of instrumental music before the Civil War without it becoming a divisive issue. After the North-South conflict, the differences couldn't be tolerated. Other religious denominations in our country divided after the Civil War. Often they would even label themselves geographically. I always took pride that the Restoration Movement didn't divide over the Civil War. But in reality, I think we divided over the Civil War and covered it up with this issue instead of admitting the real reason. It sure sounds nobler to divide over a doctrinal position rather than a political one (especially one that had emotional ties to slavery).

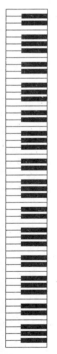

People divide over issues they are most emotional about. Perhaps you have experienced a divisive family disagreement in your past that can still bring up immense emotional reactions when it is mentioned even though many years have passed since the original argument. Since instrumental music became the focal reason for our division, we are probably more emotional about this one issue than any other. Sometimes it seems that I can stir up people more with this issue than if I were to deny the deity of Christ. Isn't it strange that an issue this peripheral can evoke more emotions and fury than any other? Perhaps we have become like the Hatfields and the McCoys. They passed on a feud from one generation to another. Yet the real reason for the feud had been lost or forgotten. Perhaps we too are divided and fighting with a group when we don't even know the real reason for it. On the other hand, it is comforting to see that much of the fighting has stopped. Clearly we recognize that the War

The Other Side of

Between the States is over, but maybe we have also begun to see that the war between the Churches of Christ and Christian Churches is over. Certainly, we are not skirmishing as much. But peace is more than a cessation of fighting as the history of the sectional divisions in our country reveals. True peace comes when there is a reunion. And it's not easy. So how do we get together? It will take some intentionality and effort, but it will be worth it. Maybe if we traveled and spent some time on the other side of the keyboard, we would discover how we are more alike than different. Perhaps we would discover more reasons to be together than apart. Even if we never discovered the real reason for the division, I'm sure we could find the reason for the reconciliation.

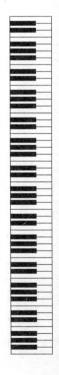

the Keyboard

Conclusion

With a lot of examination and prayerful thinking, I believe that it is fine if you prefer a cappella music. If you want to be a cappella because that is your tradition, I think that is totally acceptable. Even if you want to say that you think churches should be a cappella because that is the way you interpret the Bible, I can live with that. But if you try to bind your belief on others or try to prohibit others from worshiping with instruments, I simply don't think you have enough Bible to do so.

I was always taught in our fellowship that if you were stuck alone on a desert island and someone dropped a Bible down from the sky, you could read it and come up with the sound doctrine we believe. I think that is true about most things. But if you read from Genesis to Revelation without some preconceived ideas on instrumental music, I don't think you could ever end up with our position.

Evangelism shouldn't be the only driving force for our change. We shouldn't change things purely to attract people. But if instrumental music is not wrong, mission is definitely a factor in our choices. Hardly anything has been touching more people and bringing them to Christ in the last two decades than contemporary Christian music. As I have openly exposed myself to contemporary Christian music and worshiped with it, I believe that it is one of the most anointed ways that God is using today to bring people to Him. I hate to see any group position itself in such a way as to miss this blessing of God.

King David recognized the convicting power of music in his day: "He put a new song in my mouth, a hymn of praise to our God. Many will see and fear and put their trust in the LORD" (Ps 40:3). Similarly, nothing speaks the gospel more effectively to young people today than music. Our fellowship is definitely having problems reaching and keeping young people. Could the reason be that we are silencing one of the greatest ways God is speaking to the young today?

I'm not proposing change simply for change's sake. But I always advocate change for the sake of the mission. I think that there will always be a place for a cappella music in my life and in our congregation. But somehow I think all of us need to find a way to change to reach others. This missional thinking truly motivated me to change. But what happened in the process is that I learned some new dimensions of worship as I learned to worship with instruments.

I understand that Churches of Christ don't want to lose their distinctives, networks, or heritage. I know that Churches of Christ usually sing better. My younger son, Jeremy, sings in a jazz choir of twelve people who recently were invited to sing at Carnegie Hall. A third of the choir goes to the Churches of Christ. They grew up singing and were better equipped for singing. I would hate to lose the beauty of our singing. But on the other hand, Jeremy is also one of the most gifted guitarists that I know. He feels that he is now able to totally use his gifts as he not only sings but also plays for God. So many young people are leaving the Restoration Movement and going to churches that really don't hold the ideals of our

The Other Side of

background. Most of them tell me that they leave because of the music. I wish we could keep the young in the Restoration Movement. At the Northwest Church we were able to keep our young people with a change in music without compromising our stance on the more central aspects of the gospel. We can still network with each other even if we don't all totally practice the same worship style. A good starting place would be to completely acknowledge each other as brothers and sisters. The ultimate would be to join together as one as the Northwest Church of Christ and Shoreline Christian Church did in Seattle. Perhaps churches could meet together sharing leadership and ministries but have different worship styles in multiple assemblies. But even if churches don't merge, couldn't we at least work together in mission efforts, evangelistic outreaches, and benevolent causes? I think a lot of walls would come down if we would start attending each other's meetings, lectures, and conferences. When we finally get to know each other again, I think that we are going to fall in love with one another. I realize that no one wants to be pushed to go against his or her conscience, but I still think that the unity Jesus desires is greater than the issue that separates us.

There is life on both sides of the keyboard. I think you will find Jesus on both sides too. Can you make an effort to cross to the other side?

Don DeWelt, the great Christian Church preacher, Bible professor at Ozark Christian College, and founder of College Press, told me about the circumstances of his "death." He was reading in his quiet time the passionate prayer of Jesus in John 17. His focus was on verses 20-24.

> My prayer is not for them alone. I pray also for those
> who will believe in me through their message, that all
> of them may be one, Father, just as you are in me and

I am in you. May they also be in us so that the world may believe that you have sent me. I have given them the glory that you gave me, that they may be one as we are one: I in them and you in me. May they be brought to complete unity to let the world know that you sent me and have loved them even as you have loved me. Father, I want those you have given me to be with me where I am, and to see my glory, the glory you have given me because you loved me before the creation of the world.

This particular part of Jesus' prayer is especially pertinent because it applies specifically to us (those who believe through the disciples' message), and the subject is unity. And did you notice how united we are to be? Jesus' prayer request is that we would be as much one as the Father and the Son are One. Now that is *one*! Have you ever tried to explain the Trinity to someone? It is a doctrine involving such a oneness that it is beyond description or human explanation. And yet that is the unity Jesus requested for us.

As Don was reading this very passage, his heart quit beating and he died. After being resuscitated and finding himself in the hospital, his first recollection was looking again at his Bible. Someone had taken the very Bible from his quiet time, brought it to the hospital and opened it to the passage he was reading when his heart stopped—Jesus' prayer for unity.

Upon examination of this passage, he believed that God had brought him back to life for one reason—to bring about unity between the Churches of Christ and the Christian Churches. He told me about his story and his dream. He started the magazine *One Body* to promote unity and inaugurated many forums for discussion and healing in the Restoration Movement.

The Other Side of

Some years later as I was studying for a sermon, God put Don on my mind. I decided to call and find out how he was doing. I was told that he had just died. After I shared my condolences, his family simply told me that Don had loved me and would want me to keep his dream alive. It's my goal to do so.

Don had crossed over frequently to my side of the keyboard. He loved my side and understood it. He had also invited me to his side of the keyboard. I fell in love with his side and also understood it. What happened? We found some beautiful music on both sides. I call it harmony.

Max Lucado, speaking at the National Missionary Convention in 2003, echoed this harmonious sentiment, and it serves as a good conclusion for this book: "It's sweet for us to all be together. I don't know what happened in 1906 when the Churches of Christ went one way and the Christian Church went the other, but like one fellow said, 'We weren't around to cause the division but we can be around to see it come to an end.' And I'm thankful to see that. I hear rumors that somebody is planning a big party for 2006 in which we're all going to be invited, and we'll bring to a conclusion that separation that God is already bringing to a conclusion. I don't know where that party is going to be, but I sure want to be there, don't you?"

Notes

1 J. W. McGarvey, *Millennial Harbinger* (Bethany: Campbell, 1864) 510-512.

2 Rick Joyner, *World Aflame* (New Kensington, PA: Whitaker House, 1996) 133-134.

3 William F. Arndt and F. Wilbur Gingrich, eds., *A Greek-English Lexicon of the New Testament and Other Early Christian Literature*, based on Walter Bauer's 4th ed., 1952 (Chicago: University of Chicago Press, 1957) 899.

4 Lucian, *The Parasite*, trans. by A.M. Harmon (London: William Heineman Ltd., 1921) 17.

5 F. Wilbur Gingrich and Frederick W. Danker, eds., *A Greek-English Lexicon of the New Testament and Other Early Christian Literature*, 2nd ed., based on Walter Bauer's 5th ed., 1958 (Chicago: University of Chicago Press, 1979) 891.

6 Tom Burgess, *Documents on Instrumental Music* (Joplin, MO: College Press, 1966) 46.

7 Frederick W. Danker, ed., *A Greek-English Lexicon of the New Testament and Other Early Christian Literature*, 3rd ed., based on Walter Bauer's 6th ed. (Chicago: University of Chicago Press, 2000) 1096.

8 Ibid.

9 "Jewish Music," http://www.templesanjose.org/JudaismInfo/song/music.htm (29 Sept. 2004).

10 E. Werner, "Music," *Interpreter's Dictionary of the Bible* (Nashville: Abingdon Press, 1984) 466-469.

11 Cyrus Adler and Francis L. Cohen, "Music, Synagogal," http://www.jewish encyclopedia.com/view.jsp?artid=1022&letter=M#3369 (October 13, 2004).

12 A similar viewpoint of mourning is seen in the Diaspora worship after the destruction of the Temple. See "Jewish Music," http://www.templesanjose.org/Judaism Info/song/music.htm (29 Sept. 2004).

13 Matt Redman, *Unquenchable Worshiper* (Ventura: Regal, 2001) 102-104.

14 Rick Warren, *The Purpose Driven Life* (Grand Rapids: Zondervan, 2002) 65.

15 Ibid., 65-66.

16 Richard Hughes, *Reviving the Ancient Faith* (Grand Rapids: Eerdmans, 1996) 48.

17 David Edwin Harrell, Jr., "The Sectional Origins of Churches of Christ," *Journal of Southern History* 30 (August 1964) 262.

18 Ibid.

19 W.E. Garrison and A.T. Degroot, *The Disciples of Christ* (St. Louis: Bethany Press, 1948) 468.

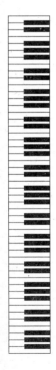